E COLLAR DOG TRAINING

The Best Guide for Everything You Need to Know About Electric Collar for Training Your Dog and Ensuring Good Behaviour

JAMES KRAMMER

Table of Contents

Introduction

E-collars, aka electronic or remote training collars, are an important part of the professional dog trainer's tool kit. Unfortunately, the many myths perpetuated about these helpful training aids have created a culture of fear surrounding what some call "shock collars."

Many of the most compassionate and ethical dog trainers in the world use electronic collars to assist them in the process. Without these tools, it would be virtually impossible to train dogs – including hunting and rescue dogs – to work off-leash.

The best way to bust these dangerous myths – and reassure dog owners about their pet's safety – is to explore the facts about electronic training collars.

Read on!

CHAPTER 1

What Is An E-Collar?

The types of e-collars used by dog training professionals are specifically designed to provide appropriate training feedback without inflicting any discomfort or pain on the animal.

Remote training collars consist of a handheld remote and a receiver attached to a collar worn by the pet. The trainer uses the remote to send a signal to the receiver at the desired time.

The myth surrounding these devices is what, exactly, the animal experiences when a signal is sent. If you've ever experienced a TENS unit when visiting a physical therapist or chiropractor, you've experienced one type of remote sensation yourself. Depending on the animal, trainers may also use vibration, tapping or audible tones to deliver a remote signal – but never a shock or another painful stimulus.

The impulses delivered by professional remote training collars cannot burn or otherwise harm the animal. What they do is send a physical signal that is safe, humane and effective.

How Do E-Collars Work for Dog Training?

When a trainer works with a dog on-leash, it's easy to provide immediate feedback when the animal displays unwanted behavior. When the dog is off his leash, however, that becomes more challenging.

Remote training collars are the ideal way to provide appropriate training feedback even when the dog is far away. In fact, some professional e-collars can signal an animal from almost a mile away!

Used correctly by professional trainers, e-collars improve a dog's confidence, well-being and safety off-leash and in a variety of field situations. They can be used for virtually all breeds and sizes of dogs.

E-Collars as a Component of a Professional Dog Training System

Many responsible dog trainers use electronic collars as a part of an overall system, along with positive reinforcement and other proven methods. These tools are used to achieve specific goals in highly controlled situations where the animal can be closely monitored.

Trainers use the lowest possible stimulus and, as in all aspects of professional training, always have your pet's health, safety and best interests in mind.

5 Common Myths About Electronic Dog Training Collars

Whether you just adopted a puppy or have an older dog, training your dog is an important step to developing a healthy life-long relationship with your canine companion. There are many methods of dog training, but one is particularly poorly understood: electronic dog training using an e-collar. Here are 5 common myths about electronic training.

Myth #1: An e-collar will hurt your dog

The stimulation provided by an e-collar is a static shock, similar to what you have probably experienced yourself on a dry winter day. It is annoying but not painful, and it is designed to get your dog's attention, it will not hurt your dog.

There are many different levels of stimulation to choose from, and you should use the lowest one to which your dog responds. Modern e-collars are equipped with safety mechanisms to protect your dog from a prolonged or dangerous shock.

You can also use audible tones and vibrations instead of the static shock setting. Used correctly, an e-collar will not hurt your dog.

Myth #2: The e-collar will burn his neck

An e-collar will not burn your dog. This myth perpetuates because when used incorrectly, the e-collar may cause pressure sores on your dog's neck.

It's important to be sure the collar is fitted correctly, and it is taken off periodically according to the manufacturer's recommendations. This will prevent any injuries from occurring due to the collar.

Myth #3: E-collar training will make your dog fearful of you

Dogs are pack animals who appreciate a strong leader. E-collars provide immediate and clear feedback to your dog, which allows them to quickly correct their behavior.

This leads to a stronger relationship with your dog. E-collars are not intended to be used as punishment or to invoke fear. You can also combine e-collar training with positive reinforcement such as treats.

When your dog is well-trained, they will respect you as a leader, not fear you.

Myth #4: Electronic training is only for hunting dogs

While this method is excellent for hunting dogs, even your backyard canine can benefit from electronic dog training collars. E-collar training works at a distance, helping to cement his skills even if you are not directly beside him.

If your dog is going to be off-leash, e-collar training can help keep him safe by allowing you to correct him even if he does not see or hear you.

Myth #5: Electronic training is hard to do

As with any dog training program, you must learn how to do it properly for it to be effective. However, using an e-collar is no more difficult than other methods. In fact, many owners find the e-collar training progresses much more quickly than other training methods.

This is because the corrections provided by the e-collar are immediate and clear, leading to less confusion for your dog.

Electronic dog training collars are prone to many misconceptions, making many people avoid it as a training method. However, e-collar training is an effective and safe way to correct your dog's behavior and train them to follow both basic and complex commands.

While no one method is going to be right for every dog, the bottom line is that e-collar training will not hurt your dog and can help you enjoy many years with your well-trained dog.

Busting of other E-Collars Myths

Like many, I once believed that e-collar training was cruel. I thought positive reinforcement was the only right way to train a dog, until I had Billy. As much as I learned and worked with him, he just wasn't as responsive to the training as I needed him to be.

As a result, I happened upon balanced training methods, thanks to friends who had faced similar difficulties with their own dogs. The more I learned, the more I saw how incredible this tool could be, when used correctly.

There are a lot of myths and assumptions out there about e-collars, and many of the claims and beliefs simply are not true. We have discussed some above but this is just to add to the list and buttress the points. This part breaks down those myths and explains the truth behind proper use of an e-collar.

Modern Day E-Collars vs Shock Collars

You've probably heard the terms e-collar and shock collar used interchangeably when referring to such tools. More often than not, the term "shock collar" is used today as a way of intentionally creating a reaction in people to associate pain and harm with its use.

The first electronic collars were introduced during the 70s, based on the psychology of shock treatment. The tools were designed to shock dogs using three different settings.

Modern e-collars use TENS technology (Transcutaneous Electrical Nerve Stimulation), which delivers a mild pulse that stimulates muscle contraction (the same thing your PT or Chiropractor uses on you when you are in for treatment).

They are also designed to safely and humanely deliver the stimulation to dogs as small as 5 lbs.

Not all E-Collars are the Same!

While the archaic shock collars of the 70s are no longer produced today, there are still a number of low quality, inhumane e-collars on the market. Nearly every trainer I have met or follow on social media use the E-Collar Technologies Mini Educator, which has a stimulation level range from 0 to 100.

How E-Collars Work

This stimulation interrupts the dog's thought process through an unpleasant, but not painful sensation.

As I will mention several times in this book, the stimulation reinforces commands the dog already knows. With proper conditioning, the dog learns how to stop the sensation by responding correctly to a command.

The e-collar can also be used to deter undesirable behaviors like digging, counter surfing, "popcorning" in the car, jumping, and more. In this instance, your dog learns to associate the unpleasant feeling with its own behavior.

Think of the e-collar as an extension of the leash. Just as your dog feels a tug on their collar when they reach the end of the leash, the e-collar is sort of like a tap on their shoulder, only does not cause damage to the larynx or spinal cord like a jerk of the collar can.

Now let's get into more myths about e-collar training!

Myth #1: E-Collars Hurt Dogs

Used incorrectly, yes, e-collars can hurt a dog.

So can a flat collar.

So can your hand.

So can a leash.

Think about your kitchen knife, a tool you probably use every day, multiple times a day.

Have you ever used that same knife to kill someone? I sure hope not.

When used correctly, a sharp knife can create delicious meals for your family. Used incorrectly, it can be a murder weapon.

Catch my drift?

Any tool can be misused. When an e-collar is used correctly, under the guidance of a professional trainer, then they are incredible tools that make life safer for your dog and give them more freedom.

Hold up. Safer? More freedom?

Yes.

I have 100% confidence that Billy will respond when I recall him back to me. Even if there is a squirrel, a dog, something tasty, a bear, you name it. I can call him off anything because of the e-collar.

Billy's working level ranges from 4 to 10 in low distraction zones. If I have to call him off something especially exciting, I might have to dial up to 30.

What this means is that I can give Billy more freedom when we hike and trail run with full confidence that he will obey commands.

Myth #2: E-Collars are for Lazy People

If e-collars are for lazy people, then I've been doing this all wrong.

I have worked with Billy on a daily basis since the day I brought him home. Those who oppose e-collars claim that having to use a tool equals laziness. What they don't proceed to recognize is that the following items are also tools:

- Collars
- Leashes
- Harnesses
- Halti's/Gentle Leader
- Food

Everything mentioned above is a tool. Everything mentioned above are tools that most trainers use.

Efficiency does not Equal Laziness

What some claim as "lazy," I call efficient. E-collars allow me to communicate with my dog in a way that they understand. They learn more quickly because the tool is more effective.

Since some of us loves to bake, let's use a baking example.

Let's say I'm making a lemon meringue pie. I can use a whisk and whip those egg whites for 20-30 minutes (or longer, trust me, I've tried it), or, I can use egg beaters for 5 minutes and save my arm strength for the gym.

Does it make me lazy to use an egg beater over a whisk? Nope. It makes me efficient. Now, I have an extra 15-25 minutes of my life back, my arm isn't wiped out, and I've got perfect peaks.

Here's a great personal example of a tool used by R+ advocates (positive reinforcement) that I consider lazy: the Halti or Gentle Leader (you can see in the name that it's all about marketing: This tool is gentle!)

We used one on Lady Bridge because she pulled on walks. Inspired by halters used for horses, the design allows the handler to control the dog's head position and helps reduce pulling. Magic!

Lady Bridge would also run away and hide every. single. time. we got out the Gentle Leader. She fought and turned her head when we'd put it on.

We didn't have to teach her how to walk without pulling because we just used the Gentle Leader.

Guess what? Billy wags his tail when I bust out the e-collar. He knows it means we're going on an adventure.

E-Collar Training Goes an Extra Step

E-collar training actually requires an extra step than positive only. Larry Krohn, one of the most well known balanced dog trainers explains his method in a Facebook post.

First, he teaches a dog a command using food and marker words. Once the dog knows that command, he introduces the e-collar, pairing it with the food and marker words.

Only when the dog understands a command is the e-collar used to both reinforce behavior or correct for non-compliance.

Myth #3: E-Collars Cause Confusion in Dogs

I found the exact opposite to be true once I began using tools like prong collars and e-collars.

When I relied on treats alone, I was only as valuable as the treats I had or I used them as a bribe. It didn't matter how much I squealed, engaged in play, walked back and forth along the same street, if I wasn't constantly shoveling food down my dog's throat, my dog would find something else more enticing.

I had no idea how to engage my dog otherwise and they had no idea what I wanted from them.

Good trainers don't just slap an e-collar on a dog and start pushing buttons believing that it will magically change a dog's behavior. An e-collar won't be introduced until a dog is fluent in a command, as explained above in #2.

What does cause confusion in dogs is asking for commands before they understand what it means, and then getting mad at them for not doing as they're told.

This is exactly what happened with a dog and I didn't understand the disconnect in our communication. I was just always frustrated with her and neither of us were in a place to work together successfully.

Myth #4: E-Collars are Used to Punish Dogs

E-collars are used to both reinforce behaviors the dog already knows, and correct when the dog does not obey or engages in an undesirable behavior using low level stimulation.

By first teaching the dog the commands, we can then use the e-collar to get the dog's attention, similar to your phone's vibration when someone is calling you.

As an example: During a hike, I call for Billy to come using his base stimulation level (about 6 out of 100). At that same moment, he's caught wind of a squirrel in the vicinity and wants to find that critter.

He hesitates on my first call, so I dial up to 10 and use the continuous button until he decides to release that pressure, and sprints back toward me so that I can re-release him to go find that squirrel.

You know that R+ training uses punishment as well, right?

What? Egad! It can't be true!

Indeed, my friends.

- Ignoring a dog that jumps on you is negative punishment.

- Withholding a treat for breaking or not performing a command is negative punishment.

- Removing access to your dog's favorite window spot because they bark at everything that goes by is negative punishment.

But, that has the word "negative" in it! That can't be right!

Negative doesn't mean "good" or "bad." Negative means "the removal of something" to discourage a behavior.

Myth #5: E-Collar Training is not Science-Based

Here's the thing with science. It changes constantly. One year, scientists prove one concept, the next, they show different results. "Scientific" studies can and do have biased results, depending on the subject.

The fact is that there are not enough quality studies on dog training that support this claim. Research shows that punishment can be effective, particularly when paired with positive reinforcement. Further, there is no evidence that shows that reinforcement is more effective and punishment can result in adverse effects.

Myth #6: You Can't Use E-Collars on Small Dogs

Um, why not?

I've seen trainers use e-collars with all kinds of dogs, ranging from chihuahuas and dachshunds to Great Pyrenese. Smaller dogs require more delicacy and size-appropriate tools, yes, but there's no reason one can't use an e-collar on a small dog.

In fact, e-collars are great tools for highly reactive small dogs who can't handle a leash correction. The e-collar lets them know that the behavior is not appropriate.

Myth #7: E-Collars Will Make Your Dog Afraid of You

The misconception is that e-collars use intimidation tactics in order to get the dog to do a behavior, but that couldn't be more incorrect.

Used incorrectly, sure. So can "non-aversive" tools.

I worked with a trainer for a dog who used a Martingale collar. When we wanted the dog to turn, we'd do a sort of snap that, when performed correctly didn't hurt, but was tricky to get right without yanking. Soon after implementing this tactic, I'd notice the dog flinching and cowering every time I went to make the snap motion.

Case in point. Improper use of any tool can make your dog afraid of you.

With proper conditioning, e-collars are wonderful tools that teach dogs how to make decisions and control the stimulation they receive.

Myth #8: E-Collars Burn Dogs' Necks

If you've ever read a book discussing the abusive traits of e-collars, then surely you've come across horrific images of dogs with "burn marks" on their necks.

These aren't burn marks. They're caused by allergies and improper use. Some dogs, including Billy, have allergies to nickel, the metal used in the contact points on my e-collar.

The manufacturer suggested I switch to the hypo-allergenic titanium contact points, and he continued to have allergies. This resulted in scabs.

I've since switched to plastic contact points and have had no issues.

The second reason you see photos of "burn marks" is a result of leaving the collar on for too long. The e-collar position must be switched every 2-4 hours, otherwise pressure sores will occur (just as humans experience bed sores when they're stuck in bed for long periods of time). A properly-fitted collar that is rotated regularly will prevent these sores.

Myth #9: E-Collars should only be used as a last resort

I don't know about you, but if I learned of a tool that expedited the learning process, bridged the bond between my dog and me, built confidence in my dog, and provided off leash reliability, I wouldn't wait to try everything else before using this tool.

I get it, it seems like a last ditch effort because you want to try positive reinforcement to see if it will work. Truth be told, not all dogs need to use an e-collar. It depends on your dog's personality and your lifestyle.

But if you enjoy hiking and trail running and going on other adventures with your dog, then why wait until you're frustrated and can't stand your dog?

Think of it like this:

You always wear your seatbelt in the car.

You purchase car, health, and home insurance, just in case.

If you live in the Northwest, you always bring a raincoat, even if the forecast shows sunny skies ahead.

I didn't get the chance to use the e-collar with my first dog and we were both miserable and frustrated. I chose to use it right away after I got Billy and we've been able to enjoy our time together nearly every day since day one.

CHAPTER 2

Still on Myths: Five Myths About Shock Collars, E-Collars, And Remote Trainers

Shock collars for dogs: either love 'em or hate 'em. There is not a lot of middle ground. What there is a lot of is myths. People have formed a lot of opinions based on the opinions of others concerning shock collars. Not too many of these opinions about shock collars are based upon first hand knowledge or fact.

Unfortunately, the most vehement opponents of the shock collars are too often those who have little to no working knowledge of a shock collar.

Myth #1: "Shock Collars Are Torture Devices"

A shock collar is a training tool which applies a negative stimulus to the dog. It can be used in the correct fashion to train a dog. It can be used improperly to cause a dog extreme pain. A leash can also be used properly as a training tool and improperly to cause extreme pain. The important word is "improperly". Used properly, a shock collar is no different than a leash as a training tool.

When you first fit a dog with a shock collar, the goal is to find the working level. The working level is the lowest level that the dog will notice. You put the collar on the dog and start at the lowest level and shock the dog. You gradually increase the level until there is a notice. Ears perked up, or the turn of the head. A yelp from the dog means it is too hot. You want to avoid vocalization. Just a "what was that" look from the dog. If the ears fall back and the tail tucks, the collar is too hot.

When using a shock collar, the key is to apply the least amount of zap needed to get the job done. Early versions of shock collars had very little means of adjusting the level of the shock. They were permanently set to "weld" and, because of this, good for very little. In contrast, modern shock collars have a huge number of levels. My shock collar has 48 levels available, all the way from imperceptible to the smallest of dogs all the way to quite hot for the most stubborn of dogs. Many levels are also useful to avoid overstepping. Overstepping is when level 5 is too little for the dog to notice and level 6 causes the dog to vocalize (which indicates that the level is too high).

Myth #2: "You Cannot Train A Hunting Dog Without A Shock Collar"

Many people who buy their first hunting dog will immediately go and purchase a shock collar. This is done because of the notion is that one cannot train a hunting dog without a shock collar. This is simply false. Hunting dogs have been trained for hundreds of years. Shock collars have only been around since the 70s.

Here is a true statement: If you do not know how to train without a shock collar, you will not know how to train with a shock collar. The shock collar is a negative training tool, but if you do not know how to use other negative training tools, the shock collar will be of no use and may cause harm to the training of the dog.

Before the shock collar, the tool of choice was the long leash, also known as the check cord. This, like the shock collar, is a tool that is used to apply negative reinforcement. The shock collar is really no different than the old school check cord.

One thing that needs to be noted: A dog can be trained for field work without using negative reinforcement. It is being done and a growing band of trainers are discarding their check cords and shock collars. A year ago I wouldn't have believed it, but the proof is in the pudding.

I use a shock collar. I am not ashamed of this fact. But, I am also making strides to use the shock collar less and less. With every dog I train I am getting smarter and using the collar less. I do this not because there is anything wrong with the collar. The fact is (agreed upon by most egghead trainers) that positive techniques stick best. I know this as fact even as I continue to train with a shock collar. My toolkit is not yet deep enough to totally discard the shock collar. But I am committed to training my animals to a higher and higher standard, and this means I have to get smarter and use less electricity.

Myth #3: "Shock Collars Are Negative...I Only Use Positive Training Techniques"

This isn't so much a myth about shock collars as it a criticism of those who oppose them in ignorance. Many trainers eschew the use of shock collars because they are a negative technique but often I find that these same trainers are using negative techniques. The loudest criticisms come from trainers who are already yanking and tugging their dogs in order to gain compliance. It is a shame because, as negative training goes, some softer dogs take to the shock collar better than the yanking and tugging from the long leash. I've seen videos of dogs being yanked and pulled and really have seen these dogs shut down, and then I've seen these same dogs blossom when trained with the shock collar. Truth be told, such a dog would be particularly well suited for a positive-only training.

Unfortunately, at this time, I've found no books available that teach gun dog training with positive-only techniques. If it existed, I would buy the first copy.

Myth #4: "Shock Collars Destroy The Relationship With The Dog"

When hunting with a hunting dog, the hunt happens not because the dog is highly obedience trained. The hunt happens because the dog and the human realize they are a team. I cannot find the birds. The dog cannot bring the birds to the ground. Hunting with a dog is a symbiotic relationship. Each party realizes that together we are better than either of us is alone. The best training one can do with their dog is to reinforce this relationship. If this relationship were to be destroyed, there would no longer be a point to maintain the relationship.

In other words, if the relationship between hunting dog and hunting human were destroyed, the hunt would cease to happen. I have hunted hundreds of times with my dog...the relationship is quite intact, in spite of the fact that I use a shock collar.

Myth #5: "Shock Collars Are A Shortcut"

This is one I heard recently, by a gentleman who has yet to finish training to completion a single gun dog. He was implying that using a shock collar was in some way cheating and a lazy way of doing things. Others have stated that it is a short cut and a means to reduce the amount of training that is required.

Using a shock collar is not cheating or is it a lazy way of training a dog. It does not shorten or hasten training in any way. In fact, in most instances, training behaviors using a shock collar looks identical to the negative-but-non-shock method. When training a dog to come when called, the first step is to train a recall using positive techniques. Treats. Later, the dog is put on a long leash or check cord and the dog is called. If the dog does not respond, the dog is reeled in or tugged on until it comes it. Now, if one is going to use a shock collar, it is only at this time that the shocking is introduced. It is overlayed on top of the reeling in or tugging. A transition is made to the shock collar. Once the transition is made to the shock collar, then the drilling begins. Repetition of the lesson is what is used to cement the lesson. The lesson needs to be repeated and proofed in all sorts of distractions. It is work, for both the pupil and trainer. If the check cord is going to be the tool of choice, then that needs to be drilled and proofed in different locations and with different distractions. The shock collar is not a shortcut. Rather it is an extra step, and regardless of the method chosen, drilling and repetition is required.

Shock collars are not the torture devices they are often portrayed to be. Nor are they the magic bullet to fix everything that is wrong with your dog. They are a tool, and in certain circumstances, this tool can be used to shape and modify dog behavior. There are other tools available as well, apart from the shock collar. Some of these are positive and some are negative. With any tool, one has to know how to use it in order for it to be effective.

CHAPTER 3

How and Why to Train Your Dog with an Electronic Collar

Some people unfamiliar with remote training collars view them as inhumane. When used correctly, nothing could be further from the truth.

Electronic training collars, or remote training collars, have been around a long time. Trainers of working dogs enforcing commands from a distance embraced the earliest models. Those early collars had limited stimulation settings, and it was not very friendly for the dog wearing it. Their utility as a training tool, however, could not be denied.

About 20 years ago, a shift happened in the training community that brought on a gentler way of training. The brand leaders of remote training collars responded, and today's collars are a product of that gentle evolution.

Are Training Collars 'Shock Collars'?

People ask me this all of the time. In person, it's easy to take the collar off of my BFF, ask the person to hold it in their hand and depress a continuous stimulation button.

At level 1, where most of my canines are, the sensation is barely perceivable. Plus, nerve tissue in a human hand is likely much more sensitive than in a canine's neck.

The reality is that the stimulation — when properly adjusted — annoys the dog, but it doesn't hurt it. I know this because I test the collars before they go on my canines every day by holding the contact points in the palm of my hand and hitting the stimulation button. The sensation might be similar to an insect crawling on your skin.

For perspective, the vibrate feature on my Garmin ForeRunner HRM watch is more of an annoyance to me than level 1 on any of my remote training collars.

When I am doing my physical training and go outside of my target training zone, my watch starts buzzing. It is annoying. I adjust my pace to turn the annoyance off, which is the same principle behind remote training collars.

As pro trainer Bill Grimmer pointed out, a remote training collar is analogous to the seat belt beeper in your car. You get in, turn on the ignition, and if you don't buckle up, the beeper goes off. It's irritating, so you buckle up to turn it off. For most of us, we now buckle up without thought. That beeper has trained us.

Why Use a Remote Training Collar?

The basis for canine training is the basis for motivating and changing behavior for humans as well – from toddlers to corporate managers. You have to establish expectations and communicate them in a way that the subject will understand. You also have to have the ability to correct behavior.

Let's say that your furry friend responds nearly 100 percent of the time when they are on a lead. Off-lead, the response isn't as dependable. If you don't have a way to reinforce the command, you are training them that it's okay to ignore you when off-lead. If you have to ask more than once, you're training them that this is a request that they may obey at their convenience. In that instance, you have zero ability to enforce the command.

Some may think using a remote collar is an authoritarian approach, and that ego is involved. Nothing could be further from the truth. What it comes down to is safety. Say, for example, you're on an outing when your dog scents and sights a deer. It takes off after the deer. There may be a busy highway a few hundred yards away, a couple of hundred feet of loose talus with huge exposure, or another person nearby may have an aggressive and dangerous canine. Suddenly, the need for a command that is obeyed 100 percent of the time becomes very real.

Martin Deeley, a professional trainer and executive director of the International Association of Canine Professionals, provided us with very rich commentary on this subject. He nicely summarized off-lead situations.

"In off leash environments, e-collars provide the ability to communicate with your dog, guiding and helping them to avoid potentially dangerous situations," Deeley said.

"Dogs in training are often over-talked, over-touched and over-excited by a trainer," Deeley added. "The e-collar allows us and the dog to be calmer, and it creates a less intrusive way to help the dog learn and make the right decisions."

With a remote training collar, you are always in the position to gently enforce a command. Getting to that point is not plug and play. There is a process that takes months of work that must be carefully followed to fully realize. It is called collar conditioning.

Remote Dog Training Collars: Get Started

Before you start collar conditioning, your pup must know its basic obedience commands. I cannot stress how important this is.

In my canine's vocabulary, there is "sit," "come," and "heel." There is no "stay." The canine is trained to "sit," for example, until told to do otherwise. These commands and the canine's response are not negotiable. I issue commands once, and if not obeyed, I enforce them. You do not ask three times.

This level of obedience allows me to take them wherever I go. If my dog bolts after a bear in Alaska, it will be a really, really bad day for everyone.

Allow me to state, again: If your canine does not know its basic commands, it is not ready for a remote training collar. If you do not know how to train those basic commands, you should enlist the services of a professional trainer – one who trains working dogs for things like search and rescue, explosives detection, and hunting.

Collar Conditioning

Collar conditioning starts well before you will ever use the collar. The first step is for your four-legged companion to recognize that at the beginning of their day, the collar goes on. It is part of their bling – nothing more. You want them to associate the collar with walks, going out, and playing. They should be used to the collar as a part of everyday life.

Remote training collars are our BFF's everyday collar. They rock a name tag, and we've marked the collars up with our contact info. I like redundancy in any critical system. The collar's power stays off unless we are training, or if we are in a situation where I might need to enforce a command.

The most important part of using a remote training collar is selecting the stimulation level. Every collar will have a variety of levels. They start at barely perceptible to the human hand and go up from there. According to Deeley, "The sensation produced should be adjusted to a level that the dog understands and accepts as part of the training communication."

When training, I adjust my dog's collar a notch tighter than usual. For the collar to work, the contact points need to be touching skin. If your canine has a long coat, your collar brand of choice will come with longer contact points that will help. My guideline for short- to medium-hair dogs is how many fingers I can slip underneath their collar. Two is good. Three fingers underneath the collar probably means that it is too loose, and the contact points are not touching the skin. It is important not to over-tighten, as the constriction can lead to muscular strain.

Sit your pup in front of you. Set the stimulation level to its lowest setting. Then, depress the continuous stimulation button on your transmitter. Work up from the lowest stimulation level, until your furry friend seems annoyed by something.

The response that you are looking for is not a yelp or pain. It will be a vibe of confusion. It will be like a fly buzzing around your BFF's head, an annoyance – nothing more. That's your baseline.

If your BFF vocalizes, if their ears go down, or if they tuck their tail underneath their body, that means the stimulation is too high. According to DVM Katie Barrowclough, canines have more muscles in their neck compared to humans. As far as nerve tissue, Dr. Barrowclough said, "[Canines] feel pain but their reactions to it are much different than humans. Dog's evolutionary tool to survival is to hide pain and act stoic to protect themselves from vulnerability, which can make it hard for us to identify their pain."

Dr. Barrowclough's last statement is important to remember when training with a remote training collar or anytime you suspect that your BFF may have sustained an injury. If you see an overt reaction, it is probably a level of discomfort that would be very unacceptable to humans. That makes it most definitely unacceptable for man's best friend.

Coming When Called

The basis of collar conditioning is that the annoyance goes away when your dog obeys you. The best way to do this is to reinforce the "come" command. As we said before, your companion must already know this command.

Grab a 20 to 30-foot piece of cord or rope. My favorite is half-inch climbing webbing. Tie a small loop in one end with a figure of eight knot, and form a noose collar at one end. This device is known as a check cord. You don't want to attach it to the remote collar. That may compromise the contact points from doing their job.

Give your BFF the "sit" command. It will be natural for your BFF to fidget. If they will not reliably sit when told, then take a giant step back in your training. You, the trainer with a superior intellect, have not fully trained your canine to sit. This is on you, not your dog.

Once the animal is sitting, back off 10 to 20 feet. Stimulate them with the continuous button at their baseline setting, while simultaneously giving the "come" command with great enthusiasm. Then, gently guide them toward you with the check cord. When they are within arm's reach, release the button. This is a time for big praise. Tell them what an awesome canine they are. Let them know, in no uncertain terms, that this is exactly the behavior that you want. As I tell people, canine training is a lot of theatrics.

The process of the canine learning to turn the annoyance off by obeying is the entire principle behind obedience training with a remote collar.

The trainer must do this process over and over in different settings. After you've done it in your yard, take them to a place with more distractions (like a playground) and repeat. Every time you give the "come" command, be prepared to issue stimulation if they do not obey. Furthermore, treat every time you issue the "come" command as a learning opportunity for your dog. As the party with superior intellect, you need to look for and anticipate these situations. Those situations are not a pain in the butt; they are awesome training opportunities.

Note that some dogs will bolt when stimulated. That is the result of the trainer teaching their pet that they can outrun the distance of the signal. This is why you work with a check cord until the only way that your dog knows to turn the annoyance off is by obeying – not bolting.

How You Should (and Should NOT) Use a Training Collar

A remote training collar is a super powerful tool because it enables you to enforce commands at a distance. This buys your BFF freedom to be off-lead– knowing that if a deer, skunk, other human, or a fast-moving dump truck come into your space, you have complete control. You have the ability to enforce a command at any distance.

Deeley nicely summarized it by saying, "The e-collar is a training tool that enhances communication, provides consistent reliable feedback even at increasing distance, and it creates a positive relationship with reduced stress between the dog and handler to help accomplish training goals."

As it is a powerful tool for good, it can also be abused. Too often, I have seen handlers and owners turn stimulation up past the place where it is an annoyance. Don't be that dog-ruining d-bag. If your canine is not responding, it's likely that your training progression has failed somewhere along the way. Take a step or two back in that progression. If you're having a bad day, don't even turn your pup's collar on. Don't let your problems tempt you to take out your frustrations on that living, breathing being that adores you.

This is your starting point. It's simply a basic tutorial for utilizing a remote training collar.

From this point, I highly recommend that you work with a trainer in your area who trains working dogs, and who trains your breed. The nuances and timing for a retriever – which has been bred to work with the handler – can be totally different for canines that were bred to work independently from the handler (like a pointer). A remote training collar will run a few hundred dollars, so budget to spend around $100 more to enlist a trainer to help you truly understand the process.

CHAPTER 4

Dog collars

Which type is best for your dog?

Every dog needs a collar, chiefly because they need something on which to hang their leash, license, ID and rabies vaccination tag.

There are so many styles of collar out there that it's easy to get one that reflects your dog's (or your) personality—but collars serve purposes beyond identification and decoration and not all kinds of collars are appropriate for all, or even any, dogs.

Read on to figure out which type of collar is best suited to your beloved pooch.

Regular collars

Flat collar

This is the standard collar for dogs. It has a buckle or plastic snap ("quick-release") closure and a ring for attaching identification tags and leash and is available in many colors and designs. A flat collar should fit comfortably on your dog's neck; it should not be so tight as to choke your dog nor so loose that they can slip out of it. The rule of thumb says you should be able to get two fingers underneath the collar.

Martingale collar

The martingale collar is also known as a limited-slip collar. This collar is designed for dogs with narrow heads such as Greyhounds, Salukis, Whippets and other sighthounds. It is also useful for a dog of any breed who is adept at slipping out of their collar or for fearful dogs who may try to retreat while out on a walk. A martingale collar is a must-have for anxious and fearful dogs.

The martingale consists of a length of material with a metal ring at each end. A separate loop of material passes through the two rings. The leash attaches to a ring on this loop. When your dog tries to back out of the martingale, the collar tightens around their neck. If the collar is properly adjusted, it will tighten just to the size of your dog's neck, without choking them. This is the most humane collar option for dogs who may slip out of their collars.

Head collar

The head collar is similar in principle to a horse's halter. One strap of the collar fits around your dog's neck and sits high on the head, just behind the ears. The other strap forms a loop around your dog's muzzle. The leash attaches to the ring at the bottom of the muzzle loop.

The head collar is good for strong, energetic dogs who may jump and/or pull. Because the halter is around your dog's muzzle, instead of their neck, your dog loses a great deal of leverage and they are unable to pull on the leash with the full weight of their body.

To be effective, the head collar must be properly fitted. As with any training equipment, the head halter is not intended to be used in a jerking or yanking fashion but rather to gently steer your dog in the direction you need them to go. Some manufacturers include instructions and a DVD with the collar. Otherwise, ask your dog trainer or a knowledgeable sales clerk for assistance with fitting. Proper fit and use should minimize the risk of injury to your dog.

It may take some time, patience and lots of treats to get your dog accustomed to wearing a head collar. Put it on them for short periods while giving your dog lots of high-value treats until your dog is comfortable in the collar. Then they should only wear it when you are taking them out on a leash. Don't leave the head collar on your dog all the time; eventually they will manage to pull off the muzzle loop and use it as their chew toy!

Aversive collars

Aversive collars, or collars that rely on physical discomfort or even pain to teach a dog what not to do, are not a humane option. While they may suppress the unwanted behavior, they don't teach the dog what the proper behavior is and they can create anxiety and fear, which can lead to aggression. Positive reinforcement training methods—ones that use rewards—are more effective and strengthen the relationship between you and your dog.

Choke chain collars

As the name implies, this collar is made of metal links and is designed to control your dog by tightening around your dog's neck, an often painful and inhumane training tool. Unlike the martingale collar, there is no way to control how much the choke chain tightens, so it's possible to choke or strangle your dog. It can also cause other problems, such as injuries to the trachea and esophagus, injuries to blood vessels in the eyes, neck sprains, nerve damage, fainting, transient paralysis and even death. It is very easy to misuse choke chains and with all the humane, effective collars on the market, choke chains are unnecessary and should not be used.

Prong or pinch collars

The prong or pinch collar is similar in design to the martingale. However, the control loop that the leash is attached to is made of chain. The loop that fits around your dog's neck is made of a series of fang-shaped metal links, or prongs, with blunted points. When the control loop is pulled, the prongs pinch the loose skin of your dog's neck. Similar to choke chains, these collars can be easily misused and should not be used.

Shock collars

Shock collars use electric current passing through metal contact points on the collar to give your dog an electric signal. This electric signal can range from a mild tickling sensation to a painful shock. Shock collars may be sold as training devices, although more and more companies are pulling them from the shelves. They are also used with pet containment (electronic fencing) systems. Shock collars are often misused and can create fear, anxiety and aggression in your dog toward you or other animals. While they may suppress unwanted behavior, they do not teach a dog what you would like them to do instead and therefore should not be used.

Electronic fencing uses shock collars to deliver a shock when the dog approaches the boundaries of the "fenced" area. Typically, the shock is preceded by a tone to warn the dog they are about to get shocked. While the dog will be shocked if they run out through the electronic fence, they will also be shocked when they re-enter, leading to dogs who are unlikely to return home.

Special use collars

Bark control collars

Though several types of collars are available to control excessive or unwanted barking, none of them address the root cause of the barking. Dogs bark for several reasons, such as fear or territorial behavior. Though some bark collars may reduce barking, they will not reduce the stress causing the dog to bark.

- **Spray:** Barking causes these collars to emit a burst of citronella or air, which interrupts and deters your dog from barking. Spray collars will sometimes not react to high-pitched barks, making them ineffective. Tip: Don't use a spray collar when your dog is with other dogs. Another dog's bark may trigger your dog's collar.
- **Ultrasonic:** When your dog barks, the ultrasonic collar interrupts them by emitting a sound only your dog can hear.

How to Get Your Dog to Stop Barking

Flea/tick collars

These collars are impregnated with chemicals and help protect your dog against fleas and ticks. They are worn in addition to a regular collar. Be sure to check how long the flea/tick collar is effective and be sure to replace it as recommended.

Vibrating collars

This type of collar uses vibration, not electric shock, to get your dog's attention. Vibrating collars can be useful to train a deaf dog who can't hear your voice or a clicker.

Elizabethan collars

The Elizabethan collar, or E-collar, is a wide, plastic, cone-shaped collar used to prevent your dog from licking or scratching wounds and/or after a veterinary procedure while they heal. Typically tabs or loops on the Elizabethan collar can be attached to your dog's regular collar. Some models have hook and loop closures to secure them. These collars come in a variety of sizes to ensure proper fit for your dog. Your dog should be able to eat and drink with the collar in place, but not be able to reach the healing site. If your dog will not tolerate an Elizabethan collar, there are other options available including soft, round collars that don't impact your dog's ability to move around or see clearly.

GPS collars

This collar uses global positioning satellite technology to help locate your pet if they get lost. While these are a great option in recovering a lost pet, they often rely on the availability of satellites and battery life, making them less effective in remote areas.

CHAPTER 5

E-Collar Conditioning

When you just purchase a new puppy it is quite easy and fun to manage him for a few weeks as he just eats, sleeps and growls at his toys. But in a few weeks, puppy starts developing his own mind and that's where things can get messy. So are you wondering at what age you should start with e-collar conditioning or teaching your small canine some manners? What is the correct time, age and manner to do so? I will give you the answers.

So, when do you start e-collar conditioning my dog? As far as training is concerned, you should introduce an e-collar to your puppy or dog from the day one you bring him home. Once the dog is settled, take small steps and take small steps to e-collar train him.

Begin with cage training, basic sit and stand or fetch command. Make each interaction with your puppy a learning opportunity and make sure he's wearing an e-collar each time as it will help him get used to the actual physical item wrapped around his neck. Continue with dog training routines such as housebreaking, controlling nuisance whining, jumping up and barking, fighting the inhibited play biting.

Best age to start e-collar training

If you are considering how old enough your dog should be for e-collar conditioning, then the truth is there are no fixed age criteria that fit for all dogs. It depends upon the condition and maturity of the dog. Some pups are ready for this training at around 14 to 15 weeks of age while for the majority of others the age should be around 6 months before you start.

So now you know at what age you should start with e-collar conditioning, but there is a lot more to it. You must also follow the correct procedure of training so that your dog remains obedient and you can take the most advantage of your e-collar. If properly trained you don't need not to remain around your dog continuously and can give it freedom too.

How to E-collar condition your dog?

There are two main principles of using an e-collar, they are:

1.   Show your dog what you want it to do.
2.   Reinforce this command with the collar.

Showing your dog what you want is collar-conditioning. This is because, before you whack up your dog, you should at least tell him what you expect. Else he would end up being scared as well as confused. But most people forget the principle of conditioning and try to correct their dogs in a way in which the dog cannot link the punishment to anything. With collar-conditioning, you can prevent that.

But it should be done with care. Here are some steps how you can do it:

1.   Show your dog what it has to do. You can start with the kennel command. You must show the dog what a kennel is by pushing it inside and repeating the command. Put the collar on the dog while doing this, but make sure that it is turned off.

2. When your dog gets a sign of understanding then you should turn the collar on. But keep it on the lowest setting meant for the dog. If it is a new dog it is good to start with 1 or 2 rather than moving to 10 or 15.

3. Turn the stimulation on first and then give the command. If the dog complies then turn off the stimulation. If he does not comply then you should force him to go into the kennel while the stimulation is still on. Once he enters the kennel then turn it off immediately.

4. Once he starts to grasp the command with stimulation then you can move to the next stage. You must do this after 1-2 weeks. Give command first and follow it with stimulation. If he complies then turn off stimulation immediately. Do this for several days.

5. Next stage is to give the command and apply stimulation only if your dog does not comply.

6. Lastly, you must generalize the command. Do this by moving the crate to different areas of your yard

or to the back of your truck. Make sure that the dog obeys the kennel command in different places.

You should not rush the process of training and let the dog learn at its own pace. With proper collar-conditioning, you lay the foundation for all future collar use. The procedure for conditioning remains the same for all commands such as sit, here, there, fetch etc. you can give commands verbally or while whistling.

Many people do good training in the yard but fail in the field and this is because of the dog's excitement. While you cannot control the dog's behavior, you can control yours. While correcting your dog, make sure to control your temper and do not give any corrections in anger.

Correct the dog only after you give proper command verbally or by a whistle and he disobeys willfully. Turning on the button again and again and activating the stimulation can make the dog irritated to a great extent. Lastly, give your pup benefit of a doubt if he makes any mistake – give him another chance and keep your thumb off the button.

Also, it might be a good time to introduce a clicker to your dog.

What is the right size of e-collar for your dog?

To know the correct size measure the size of your dog's neck in inches and measure the size from neck to the snout. Here is a guide to finding the most appropriate size for your canine.

X-Small: Neck Size = 8"-10", Cone Length = 4"

Small: Neck Size = 12"-14", Cone Length = 6"

Medium: Neck Size = 13"-15", Cone Length = 8"

Large: Neck Size = 15"-17", Cone Length = 10"

Can your dog sleep while wearing the e-collar?

You can allow your dog to sleep with the e-collar on his neck, but if the pup is not comfortable with the new hardware, and then you should not force it to wear while sleeping. It all depends on personal preferences and comfort of your dog.

Second opinion on What Age to Start E-Collar Training?

You recently acquired a new puppy and other than the middle of the night potty breaks, the first few weeks were pretty easy. The pup mostly ate, slept, gently gnawed on his toys, and waddled along a few feet behind you, never getting too far from sight.

But a few weeks have gone by and that devoted pup has suddenly developed a mind of his own. He is darting into the street to chase squirrels, chewing on the corner of the sofa, and using those piranha-like incisors to clamp down on your hands when you try to pet or brush him.

You're wondering if you can use dog obedience collars to start teaching better manners but a friend who has trained a few of his own dogs has told you he is too young. In fact, the more people you ask, the more conflicting opinions you get!

It is fairly common knowledge that you should start training your puppy as soon as he comes into your home.

Our dogs are taking in information all the time. Each interaction with them is a learning opportunity and basic manners like housebreaking, learning to inhibit play biting and control of nuisance whining, barking and jumping up should start young. It is ideal if the pup grows up never really having learned and ingrained bad behaviors to begin with.

But when it comes to the question of how old is "old enough" to start using an e-collar to train a dog, the truth is, there isn't a one size fits all answer. Some pups are ready to go around 14 or 15 weeks of age, others should be close to the typically standard prescribed 6-month old time frame before you start.

If your pup is large enough to fit the collar properly AND has an outgoing, boisterous type of personality, you can very likely add an e-collar to the training tool kit and get started earlier than you would if you have a quiet, reserved pup. The more withdrawn puppies should have extra attention paid to exploring the world and experiencing a spectrum of positive adventures rather than focusing on reining them in too soon and creating potential hesitancy.

My personal belief is that the decision about e-collar training should depend on a factor far more important than the age of the dog. A factor that is even more important than the dog's overall temperament.

In my opinion, the decision should be weighted heavily on you as the operator, your knowledge of the tool, and very importantly, your willingness to put in the needed training time. If you're a patient person, willing to learn to use the collar properly (or you're already experienced) you can get started. On the other hand, if you're only looking for a quick fix to punish nuisance behavior (and not take the time to teach the dog what to do) you should reassess your motivation and the relationship you have with your dog.

If both you and your dog are ready, then go for it and get busy with the collar conditioning protocols and do the work.

Put in the practice sessions because collar conditioning teaches your dog HOW to properly respond and have control over the sensation. That understanding will bring a happy working attitude rather than a sullen or deflated one and you'll end up improving the relationship you have with your dog and more thoroughly enjoying your time together.

The thing that will vary based on your dog's age, is how much work you can do in a given session and for how long. Pay attention and honor the limitations of your dog's attention span when you start. Err on the side of caution and keep your sessions short, rather than too long. You will build your dog's mental endurance as you practice together. And focus on what is going right; help your young dog get it right. Don't be stingy with the use of rewards and praise.

Once the dog understands how to respond and do as you ask, everything else will begin to fall in line. You will have a well-mannered, happy dog and you will be able to enjoy more adventures together.

Third Opinion on Age to Start

When it comes to donning e-collars on dogs, more often than not, you will wonder at what age should E-collar training start.

This is especially true if you have a puppy. On the most instruction manual for E-collars, they will state that the E-collar should only be used on dogs who are at least 6 months in age. But how true is this, or perhaps there are other guidelines that will determine at what age should e-collar training start?

Here's what it is, the age of the dog should only be a small part of the bigger picture. There are indeed other factors that you will need to consider other than age. True enough; puppies below 6 months of age might not be suited for e-collar training as they might not be adequately developed to appreciate training processes as well as the corrections that come with the e-collars. More importantly, there are several other factors that you should be mindful of when you start the e-collar training in your dog.

Age of dog

The age of the dog should be the first indication that you should look out for when you want to start e-collar training. For starters, we completely agree that dogs below the age of 6 months should not be exposed to e-collars. This is because, atthe young age, they might not have the ability to receive training or to receive the various types of stimulation.

Dog's temperament

Apart from the age of the dog, you should look deeper into the dog's temperament. This is one aspect that most dog owners ignore, which will have a disastrous effect on your dog should events go awry.

There are various temperaments that you will need to be mindful of, especially when you are just about to start e-collar training on your dog. For example, dogs who have a milder temperament might be adverse towards starting e-collar training at a younger age. Also, should the dog react negatively, it will cause long-term effects onto the dog's characteristics.

Similarly, if the dog is aggressive in nature, you might want to be extremely careful when handling them during the e-collar training phase, as their aggressive nature might mean that they are tougher to handle.

Appropriateness of stimulation type

For e-collars, there are typically three main types of correction. Each of them is suited for different types of temperament, so it all links up!

- **Shock Stimulation:** For shock stimulation, the e-collar will emit a correction when the trainer press the stimulation button. The shock is harmless and indeed safe for dogs. All PetSpy e-collars have varying levels of stimulation so that you can choose the proper for your dog. Usually, dogs that are aggressive in nature, as well as older dogs, might be more receptive to this type of correction.

- **Vibration stimulation:** If your dog is younger and timid in nature, then you can consider using a vibration stimulation.

- **Tone Stimulation:** If your dog is extremely timid or he is very young, you can consider using tone stimulation.

Hence, after this, what is the appropriate or best age to start e-collar training on your dog? It depends on the above-mentionedfactors. Most importantly. It will also be determined byyour readiness to train your dog patiently.

The recommendation is to purchase an e-collar and let your dog wear it for a few days without administering any stimulation. Once your dog does not reject the e-collar, you can start the training properly!

CHAPTER 6

Reasons to Use an E Collar to Train Your Dog

Are you having trouble training your dog? No matter how much you love your canine companion, unwanted behaviors can leave you feeling at your wit's end. Whether your dog is Incessantly barking, chewing valuable property, running away, jumping up, or just not obeying your commands, there is an easy answer to solving it with a remote training collar.

While you may have resistance to using a remote training collar on your dog, they're preferred by professional trainers because they're the fastest and easiest way to break undesired behaviors.

It's important to make the distinction that you are not shocking your dog out of frustration, nor are you hurting your canine.

When used the right way, remote training collars give you a way to instantly communicate with your dog, from a distance, using light attention-getting stimulation or vibration.

1. Provide better communication with your dog

Dogs need clear and instant feedback from their owners. Instead of yelling and being frustrated, the remote training collar creates a bridge allowing you to better communicate with your dog. When your dog has clear and consistent communication from you, it takes far less time to train them.

2. Give your dog instantaneous feedback

A remote training collar gives you a way to provide your dog with instant feedback. Why is that important? Your dog wants to please you, but their attention span isn't as great as yours. A remote training collar gives you a way to interrupt naughty behaviors as they're happening, even when your dog is a distance away from you. This helps them understand what they're doing wrong in the moment, which is far easier on the dog. It also means that they can learn faster.

3. Quickly give your dog off-leash freedom

When you've been dealing with undesirable behaviors, trusting your companion dog to be off-leash may seem like an impossible dream. But a remote training collar is the quickest way to safely transition your dog to off-leash freedom. You'll be able to confidently allow your dog to roam on your hike in the mountains, beach or campsite within weeks. The remote training collar will allow you to maintain control, communication and keep your dog safe.

4. Reduce your stress and frustration

Training a dog can be challenging and frustrating. But when used correctly a remote training collar dramatically reduces the learning curve for your dog. You should see results in the first couple of remote collar training sessions. Your dog's quick change in behavior will take the stress out of training, leaving you feeling empowered again.

5. Increases your dog's success rate

Dogs want to follow and please the pack leader. When they receive clear communication about their undesired behaviors, they're learning how to please you. These successes breed a desire to please you further. Your dog will be ready to learn more. Before you know it, you'll be successfully teaching your dog more advanced lessons and tricks.

These are just five of the many reasons to use a remote training collar to train your dog. Once you begin using a remote training collar to train your dog, you'll find even more advantages to using them.

They take the stress out of dog training and help you maintain a healthy relationship with your dog. Don't waste time on futile training techniques. Trust the technique professionals rely upon to help you have a well-behaved, happy dog.

How to Stop Dog Chasing with an E Collar

Dogs are natural predators, so when they see something move their urge is to chase it. When it comes to chasing, this instinctual urge can be harmful or even fatal if the dog should become lost or dart into traffic. In this post, you'll learn how to use an e-collar with low-level stimulation and the "tapping method" to stop dog chasing.

There are other training methods to solve this type of behavior, however, using an e collar is a proven, sure-fire way to stop dog chasing quickly and safely from a distance.

Using an e-collar to stop unwanted behavior such as chasing relies on a technique called positive aversion training. Essentially this means when your dog is engaged in unwanted behavior, such as chasing a squirrel, you use the e-collar to introduce an unpleasant association. With consistency, your dog will begin to relate chasing with the unpleasant feeling, taking the joy out of the chase.

Educator e collars are unlike many others on the market. Lower quality Asian brands use only 10-15 levels of stimulation and outdated "sharp pulse" technology, which can be painful and cause head jerking. Educator e collars are manufactured in the USA and use the latest technologies including vibration, tone, and 100 levels of gradual medical grade "wide pulse" stimulation. This stimulation is similar to a TENS machine and feels like someone flicking the side of your neck with a finger – annoying, but not painful.

Safety Tips

Before you begin using your e collar to eliminate chasing behavior, take the time to review these safety tips:

- Always train your dog in a safe area. This may mean keeping your dog on a long leash line well away from traffic or training in a fenced area.

- Use the lowest stimulation level that gets your dog's attention. Your goal is never to hurt your dog, but rather to pull their attention away from the unwanted behavior. With chasing, you may need to use a stronger stimulation than for other behaviors if your dog has a strong prey drive.

Stop Your Dog Chasing Cats & Other Animals

If your dog can't resist chasing a passing cat or squirrel, you can quickly stop this chasing behavior with the e collar following these steps.

1. Locate a safe area where there will be many opportunities for your dog to chase.
2. Fit the e-collar on the dog and set it to the predetermined lowest level your dog responds to.
3. Keeping the dog on a long lead or in a fenced area, allow your dog to begin to chase.
4. As soon as the chase begins start tapping on the stimulation control repeatedly until your dog stops chasing. For dogs with higher prey drives you may need to gradually turn up the stimulation dial while tapping until your dog stops chasing.

During this process, do not give any verbal commands. Your dog should associate the chase with the stimulation, not with you. By repeating this process every time your dog begins to chase, he will soon learn that chasing results in an unpleasant sensation and stop chasing.

Using the vibration or tone modes on the e collar as a warning will quickly teach him to stop chasing with just the vibration or tone, without any stimulation.

Stop Your Dog Chasing Cars

Vehicle chasing is extremely dangerous for dogs. The training is very similar to eliminating animal chasing. Enlist a partner who can ride a bicycle or drive very carefully past your dog and follow the above steps. Because of the importance of stopping this behavior, make sure you are careful with the timing and strength of the correction.

By following these simple steps you can quickly and safely stop dog chasing, keeping your pet and other animals safe.

CHAPTER 7

What Causes A Dog to Chew & How to Train

Them to Stop with an E-Collar

Has your little darling gnawed the leg off grandma's antique dresser? Have you come home to find shoes chewed to shreds and blankets or other articles of clothing looking like swiss cheese?

When our pets destroy valuable objects it can be frustrating and create negative emotions that can lead to inappropriate discipline. Destructive chewing is probably the one behavior that every dog owner faces at some point.

Before addressing what to do, it is important to understand that dogs love to chew. Regardless of what it may feel like, it's not personal; your dog is not chewing to tick you off. It is completely natural for dogs of all ages to interact with the objects in their world by mouthing or chewing on them.

Why Puppies Chew

If your pet is still a puppy, then his chewing is due to teething. Between four and six months is when pups lose their baby teeth and get their adult teeth.

Just like in humans, it can be painful, so your pup will seek relief. Chewing on things feels good and offers momentary relief. Things with corners or made of wood seem to be especially soothing to pups.

First off, you must accept that you will not stop your pup from chewing; he must chew and cannot control the urge. Remember, it feels really good to the pup whose gums and teeth hurt during the teething period.

Also, never punish your pup for chewing, especially after the fact. He will not understand why you are punishing him; dogs do not relate punishment now with an act done previously. Punishment will only cause confusion and may backfire on you causing your pet to fear you which will impact all training and your future relationship with him.

That said, there are solutions for puppy chewing. The first is to give your pup something appropriate to chew: bones, toys, teething rings, even ice cubes can be used.

At first he won't know the difference between what can and cannot be chewed. You must be observe your pup at all times and the minute he starts to chew something forbidden, calmly say "no" and take it away, then immediately replace it with something he can chew and praise him lavishly when he does.

You must do this diligently. You are not trying to teach your pup that chewing is bad, but rather that chewing is not allowed on certain objects, but chewing on his toy is a good thing that will bring praise and reward.

You will find that you have to buy a lot of bones and chew toys during these two to four months, but trust that the phase will pass, and when it does your pup will have developed good habits regarding what he can and cannot put his mouth on. Crate or confine Wags when you cannot chaperon, and be sure to leave plenty of chewables for him.

Why Adult Dogs Chew

In adult dogs, destructive chewing is a symptom of other problems. The most common reason a dog chews is because he is lonely and bored.

Canines are intelligent, social creatures; it is unnatural for a dog to be left alone for long stretches of time. High energy dogs will be even more likely to resort to destructive behaviors, when left alone, so you must provide adequate exercise and stimulus for him.

There are several ways to entertain Wags, but the best solution is to simply give him more attention, more/longer walks, more play time, and more toys.

Sometimes a second pet, or play companion can alleviate the problem. You may need to take your dog to doggy daycare, or arrange for walker to visit during the day to exercise Wags.

This can be an expense, but it will surely be worth it.

Destructive chewing is not a behavior that will go away on its own; on the contrary it will likely escalate into a bigger problem.

Problem Chewers

There are instances where a pet owner finds herself with a dog – perhaps a rescued dog or one adopted as an adult – who has already developed a serious chewing habit.

Sometimes Wags simply decides that nothing is as satisfying as the piano leg. If your dog has selected a single object as a favorite chew "toy" there are products to repel the dog.

Products such as Bitter Apple or other awful tasting sprays can be applied to the desired object. More commonly though, the dog is chewing anything he can to relieve boredom and excess energy.

The Solution – Training with an E-Collar

If all else fails and no amount of exercise or toys will stop Wags from gnawing on the wrong objects, you may want to try an electronic dog collar (E-collar).

Using an e-collar to prevent your dog from biting and chewing is a great solution. E-collars come with a remote control that creates an electric stimulation. You might think this sounds torturous or cruel, but for chronic problem behaviors they can be the most humane choice. Most e-collars come equipped with variable intensity to insure that you dog not overstimulate or hurt your pet.

Contrary to what you may read online, E-collars are a sure-fire way to solve dog behavior problem safely and humanely. When used responsibly electronic collars can be the most effective method to eliminate behaviors such as destructive chewing, jumping up, running away and other unwanted activities.

How to Use An E-Collar to Stop Chewing & Biting

The first rule of using a shock collar for biting and chewing issues is to use only lowest setting to which your dog responds. Most dogs require only minimal stimulation, but pain thresholds are individual, and every dog has his limit.

Another consideration in setting the intensity level is the degree of distraction. You may need to adjust the stimulation if Wags is distracted. You want your dog to respond, but not jump or yelp; the idea is to interrupt or startle Wags, not hurt him.

Once you determine the appropriate level, you will select the continuous function on your e'collar. This function produces stimulations until you disengage the trigger.

For training what you do not want your dog to do, such as chewing on the piano, this is the best method. Outfit Wags in the collar and then allow access to the object he desires to chew.

The instant he begins chewing on it, begin to tap on the trigger. Wags should immediately drop the object or stop chewing, when he does, stop tapping immediately.

Timing is crucial. Wags will likely learn very quickly that to stop the annoying sensation, he needs to stop chewing on the piano. If he doesn't respond, you may need to increase the stimulation a step.

But be careful with this;

Before choosing to purchase an e-collar assess your dog's behavior carefully. If you are a first time dog owner or unsure why your dog is exhibiting destructive behaviors, do some research and consult professionals. If you determine that he may be chewing because of separation anxiety, hire a professional dog trainer or behaviorist.

Electronic collars, though safe and effective for use on healthy adult dogs, are not recommended for dogs with psychological problems. E-collars are never a good choice for puppies, tiny dogs, shy, fearful or stressed dogs and should never be used to punish your pet indiscriminately.

CHAPTER 8

Common E-Collar Mistakes and How to Avoid Them

When properly used an Electronic collar, or E-Collar, is, in my opinion, one of the best tools you can use to train and handle a patrol dog. When used incorrectly it can be one of the worst tools in our arsenal. I have trained hundreds of dogs all around the country on the proper use of an E-Collar and see many of the same mistakes. I share these ideas to assist you in looking at your own training to see if you too are guilty of any of these common E-Collar mistakes.

Be sure to check out our excellent stock of high-quality K9 Electronic Collars for even the toughest police and military dogs.

Common Mistake #1

Not having a written policy for using E-Collars

An E-collar is a powerful tool and it should be regulated by proper department policy. Without such a policy there is a risk of misuse or even abuse by improper E-collar use. By having a clear policy outlining the proper use of an E-Collar an agency is protecting itself as well as its officers. The policy should, at a minimum, include how the E-collar will be used in training and on the street. It should define who is authorized to teach the proper use of the E-Collar. It should explain where the E-collar is to be placed on the dog (neck only). The policy should mention if the use of the E-Collar is mandatory or an elective, leaving the handler some discretion for work and training. The policy should define a standard for handler training in the use of the E-collar prior to its full use.

Common Mistake #2

Not having sufficient training before using an E-Collar

When handlers have not been trained in the proper use of the E-collar and don't have a solid foundation for the dog training techniques that incorporate the use of an E-collar, many problems can and generally do begin to develop.

Some of the problems misuse of an E-Collar can lead to are: inconsistent performance by a dog, handler aggression from the dog, a dog that will fail to engage and or release early, a dog that will not search properly and the most common problem - a dog that will only be obedient when wearing an E-Collar. It sometimes amazes me when I see a department has dealt with one or more of these issues for long periods of time and yet continues to use the E-Collar in the same way. The good news is that proper use is not hard and can be learned in just a few days with proper instruction. Canine behavior problems that are noted and addressed in their early development, stemming from improper E-collar training, can oftentimes be corrected with only a few training sessions and with little conflict. Solidified behaviors can sometimes be more difficult to modify in terms of time, technique and repetition.

Common Mistake #3

Being intimidated by the E-Collar

When I teach E-Collar classes I always start out with a classroom lecture to outline the basics. I start the class by asking for a volunteer that I can use the collar on. Not surprisingly, I do not get many volunteers. Often I am greeted with either laughter or fear from handlers who are convinced that they cannot endure the stimulation that the E-Collar emits. I find it troubling that many times we do not think twice about putting the collar on our dogs and yet are terrified of it ourselves. I believe in order to properly use the collar a handler has to know what the stimulation feels like. The first part of any E-Collar training should include each handler feeling the stimulation (at a low level) and understanding its effects.

Common Mistake #4

Teaching the dog to become Collar Dependent

When used properly as a shaping device, a dog's performance will be the same whether wearing an E-Collar or not. We have all seen the dog that performs perfectly with an E-Collar on and is an inattentive mess without one. That is the definition of 'Collar Dependent.' How do we avoid that problem? First, it is important to neutralize the feel of wearing the collar to the dog. The Collar has a unique feel to the dog; the mere weight of the device alone is different in addition to the prongs. It is best to have your dog wear the Collar for varying times for several days or even weeks before the Collar is turned on. This will help keep the dog from pairing the unique feel of the Collar to the stimulation. Trainers who put a collar on a dog and immediately subject the dog to high levels of stimulation will train the dog to behave better when the collar is on. My goal is to shape the dog properly and have consistent behavior with or without the E-Collar.

Common Mistake #5

Testing the dog instead of shaping with the Collar

In addition to not doing any foundation at the beginning, the most common mistake I see in training the dog to become Collar Dependent is to not pair the command with the stimulation simultaneously. Using the release, as an example: if the dog is given the command and then the handler waits 1-2 seconds before applying stimulation with the collar, he has just taught the dog to wait to see if the collar is on before he releases the bite. If the stimulation is paired with the command during training it will shape the dog and keep him from testing the collar. The verbal command then becomes the prompt, to which the dog will respond.

Common Mistake #6

Using the E-collar as a short term 'fix' to a problem

Let's face it, we have all seen the times when a dog is not releasing properly and the certification is in the next few days. How many times have we seen the collar come out and used as punishment to 'try to get the dog through the cert'? I can tell you that if for some reason that short term fix works, it will create long term stress on the dog and create many more issues down the road. Training needs to be an ongoing process and not designed to try to make up for a year of missed training the night before a certification. Each handler should have their own assigned E-collar and it should be a consistent piece of training and deployment equipment. It shouldn't be a borrowed gadget as part of a smoke and mirrors magic show by which you hope to veil a temporary passing performance over an ever-persistent set of canine control issues. Learn to use the E-collar to maintain proper performances. There are no quick fixes in E-collar dog training.

Common Mistake #7

Using the Collar for "everything"

My favorite part of teaching proper E-Collar classes around the country is when the idea of shaping and not punishing clicks with both the handler and the dog. On the third day of the class, we do scenarios that were unthinkable just two days earlier. For instance, we do an exercise with six or more decoys in suits on a baseball field and direct the dog to different locations all from the pitcher's mound.

Dogs that would not recall or release two days earlier will release from 50 yards away and follow the handler's direction. The success can be a double-edged sword; I have had handlers get so excited about the success that they have approached me with ideas to use the E-Collar for training in ways that are not appropriate. For example, one handler was so happy with the progress he made at the class he emailed me later and wanted to know how to use the E-Collar to keep his dog's nose down on a track. I saw the dog track and he was excellent, but the handler thought he should keep his nose lower for some reason and was interested in how to use the E-Collar to do so.

I share this story as a way to show how seductive success with the E-Collar can be. I caution that while it is a great tool, it has to be used properly. I can only imagine what type of problems and bizarre behaviors that handler would have created if he would have started to stimulate the dog with the E-Collar while the dog was tracking.

With proper training, a good foundation and sound understanding of the E-Collar, you will be able to take your training to a much higher level.

CHAPTER 9

Difference Between E-Collar vs. Shock Collar

As a pet parent, dog trainer, or dog walker you are probably wondering what the controversy is regarding an e-collar vs. shock collar. The word shock often surprises consumers who have their dog's best interest at heart. No pet parent or caring animal lover wants to cause harm to any animal especially not their beloved furry family member. It's important that you learn the differences between a shock collar and an e-collar so you can make the right choice for your dog.

What's the difference between an e-collar and a shock collar?

Chances are you probably heard the term e-collar and shock collar used within the same sentence and referring to the same object. E-collar stands for an electronic collar and shock collar is just another way of defining the e-collar.

The term shock collar was publicly used to attempt to deter consumers from using the collar. Animal activists have expressed their concern regarding e-collars and conveniently use the word shock to scare people away from the products. No one wants to shock or physically hard their dog. When an e-collar or shock collar are used correctly, they do not harm your dog.

You might be wondering what is the difference between an electronic collar, e-collar, and shock collar. The truth is that it's virtually all the same product, but it just has different names that are used by different people. However, technically there is no difference between the two terms that are often used interchangeably.

Since there isn't a difference between an e-collar and a shock collar there really is no debate or difference between the two. However, the following information will help you learn more about the e-collar and how it will benefit you and your dog and in a safe way.

History of the E-Collar vs. Shock Collar

Electronic collars were introduced in the 1970s with the intention to use shock treatment as behavior modification for dogs. Today, the e-collars available in the market use electronic stimulation the causes a vibration to alert your dog to correct their behavior, not electrocution.

Basically, the vibration stimulates nerves and sensory receptors that distract your dog from their current behavior and help you use the e-collar as a beneficial and safe training school. As the result, your dog does not experience any pain. However, they do feel an annoyance and discomfort at a humane level.

Are E-Collars safe for dogs?

Yes. E-collars are safe to use on dogs when used properly. Electronic and shock collars work by activating then nociceptors also known as skin receptors that detect pain. When an e-collar is in a low or medium setting and is activated your dog perceives the electronic stimulation as if it were a small prick to the skin surface. The prick has been identified to be similar to a flea bite.

However, if an e-collar is misused at higher levels and activated frequently the sensation would no doubt feel harsh but won't cause physical damage to the surface of the skin. It's recommended that you start on the lowest of shock settings and see if your dog reacts to the shock. You can gradually increase the shock of your collar until your dog starts to react.

When looking at the topic from a physical standpoint, e-collars are definitely safe to use on dogs when the pet parent follows directions properly.

Are E-Collars cruel?

E-collars do inflect the perception of pain and raises ethical concerns with animal activists and some pet parents who are doubting the use of the product. Generally, e-collars are used as a last resort to help train an aggressive dog that has failed to adhere to other training methods.

E-collar training is a negative reinforcement training technique that requires the pet parent, dog trainer, and other users to use and stick to a moral compass.

Reports have revealed that negative reinforcement training is a proven and effective technique that drives a point across to the dog to help stop the aggressive behavior and prevent it from continuing.

As a parent, it's up to you to determine if the use of an e-collar is ideal for training your dog and their specific behavior.

How to Use an E-Collar to Train Your Dog

As a dog owner, you should always choose to begin training your dog with verbal commands and rewarding good behavior with treats. However, there are very stubborn and difficult dogs to deal with that require additional training techniques that include using an e-collar.

E-collars are usually used to correct antisocial behavior such as jumping on people, excessive barking, nipping, growling, and chewing household items. Some dogs also express aggressive behavior by lunging at other dogs and humans.

The following techniques will help you use an e-collar to train your dog and correct their negative behavior:

- **Allow your dog to get comfortable wearing the e-collar** – E-collars are meant for temporary use but it's important that you allow your dog time to become comfortable and familiar with wearing the collar before you put it to use. Allow your dog to wear the collar for up to five days before you begin using it as a training tool.

- **Use the lower settings first** – Always begin using the lower settings first and gradually increase the settings only if needed. The majority of dogs only need the lowest setting for the caller to be effective and successful. Avoid using higher settings and if it comes to that point you should consult with a professional trainer or veterinarian before doing so.

- **Avoid letting your dog see you use the remote for the collar** – E-collars have a remote that allows you to control your dog's behavior. Since the e-collar causes discomfort and a prick feeling to the surface of the skin you want to avoid letting your dog see that you are the one causing the discomfort. Aggressive dogs that realize their owner is causing the discomfort will often attack to prevent the discomfort from continuing.

- **Train your dog effectively and safely** – E-collars quickly and effectively teach your dog commands even in intense and aggressive situations. Always ignore your dog when they are not following your directions but praise them when they adhere to your commands. A small treat and pat on the head is an excellent way to reward your dog for their good behavior such as stopping there barking, chewing, and other bad habits.

Correcting Uncontrollable Behavior

All dogs learn new behaviors and commands at their own pace. Highly aggressive and uncontrollable behavior may take longer than you expect. As a pet parent or dog trainer, you need to be patient and kind when training your dog. It's essential that you use verbal commands when possible to coincide with activating the e-collar.

Always use your best judgment when activating the e-collar. For example, if your dog is exhibiting potentially damaging behavior that could harm them such as running out into the middle of a street or chewing on an electrical cord that can cause electrocution or even death make sure you act promptly using the proper setting. A popular method of using the e-collar is a 3 quick push on the remote technique for emergency situations.

This means you would quickly activate the e-collar three times to immediately grab the attention of your dog. This technique is only recommended and extremely deadly and dangerous situations. Otherwise, activating it once is usually all you need to correct your dog's behavior.

Always avoid misusing the shock collar to ensure your dog remains healthy and happy. Make sure your dog never finds out that you are the one activating the collar because it can cause an aggressive dog to feel more angry, scared, fearful, and distrusting. Basically, it can ruin your close bond with your dog. Always behave in a humane and loving way when using the collar.

Benefits of Using an E-Collar on Your Dog

Using an e-collar on your dog is highly beneficial when done properly. Keep in mind that the shock or electronic collar is a tool used for training purposes and once your dog has learned to correct their behavior the e-collar should not be used any longer.

Surely as a responsible pet parent, you have experienced times when your dog has chewed on the furniture, run out the front door towards the middle of the street, dug holes in the backyard, jumped on visitors when you open the front door, and behaved negatively in a variety of different ways.

Understand that a dog's negative behavior is often learned because they are allowed to continue being this way. As a dog owner, you have to power to help your dog behave in a good way.

Using an e-collar gets the job done that wasn't able to be completed with general dog training techniques. Some highly aggressive dogs are very difficult to stop and some pet parents have reported being bitten or lunged towards by their own dog or the other dog involved in an aggressive situation.

The shock collar is beneficial to dog owners because it prevents you from needing to physically interfere between two aggressive dogs. The e-collar collar is run by remote and can be used without your dog's knowledge in combination with verbal commands.

Dog owners often report successful endings when using an e-collar for training purposes. In the end, a few moments of discomfort that result in improved behavior and living happily with your dog while maintaining a strong bond is one of the incredible benefits of using an e-collar.

If you have used an e-collar properly for six weeks or more and your dog has not shown improvements in their behavior it's best to contact a professional dog trainer for further guidance.

Conclusion for E-Collar vs. Shock Collar

There's virtually no difference between an E-collar vs. Shock Collar. It's more of a terminology debate that was bought to light by animal activists who would prefer not to shock their dogs. However, using an e-collar or shock collar correctly doesn't actually hurt your dog. Always start with the lowest shock settings and gradually work your way up. This is a great way to train really stubborn dogs.

CHAPTER 10

Shock Collar For Your Dog: Finding The Right Level

A modern shock collar often has stimulation levels that range from "not noticeable" to "able to light Wichita". How do you know what level to use on the dog? Good question. I am here to help.

Here is the high level summary of finding a good level

1. Put the shock collar on yourself

2. Have the dog wear the collar

3. Recognizing a good level

Put The Collar On The Human

Probably the most important thing you need to do is put the shock collar on yourself. Put the prongs on your hand or strap it onto your calf or thigh. If you are unwilling to experience the stimulation yourself, you have no business delivering the stimulation to your dog. Knowing what it feels like will make you less likely to increase the stimulation level. It will give you a steady hand.

When you put the collar on yourself, you will want to start with the lowest stimulation level possible. Start low and slowly build up. Take note of the level when you can barely feel it, when it is noticeable, and when it hurts. This range will not be the same for your dog, but it will be similar. If you cannot handle a level above 4, and you are delivering a level 18 to your dog, something is wrong.

Put The Collar On The Dog

Once you have felt the stimulation yourself, go ahead and put the shock collar on your dog. Here is an entire article on how to do that. The best thing you can do after putting the collar on the dog is to just have him wear it. No stimulation. Nothing. Just have him wear it for a while to get used to it. Have the dog wear the collar during fun times. Like going for a walk. Make sure the collar is turned off and you leave the transmitter at home. I'd do this twice or three times or so...no hard and fast rule though.

Find A Good Level

Once he is used to wearing the shock collar, the next step is to find a good stimulation level for the dog.

You want the dog to be somewhere where his attention is not fixed on you. Keep the dog close to you so you can observe him. Set the level to the absolute lowest stimulation level possible, and deliver a stimulation. If you have a quality collar with a lot of levels, chances are good that the dog will not notice it. Increase the stimulation level by the smallest increment possible and deliver the stimulation again. Watch your dog's reaction.

You are looking for some sort of reaction. An ear twitch. A turn of the head. Some subtle change in the dog's behavior. You are not looking for a yelp. You are not looking for pain. You are looking for something that indicates that the dog felt it. Sometimes the reaction is subtle, so go ahead and give the stimulation again. Did you see it again? If so, this is the operational level at which you will start your training.

The goal is to find the level that the dog will respond to, twice. The response is an ear twitch or a turn of the head. You start at the absolute lowest level and increase until you see the subtle response twice.

Take note of this level. This is your dog's starting training level. Burn this level into your brain. This is the start. The most important rule is this: You want to use the lowest effective level to reinforce a known behavior.

CHAPTER 11

Things to Know Before Buying a Shock Collar

Whether you have a pup with a penchant for persistent barking, or you'd like to train your dog to stay in the yard, you may have considered a shock collar (aka electronic collar, e-collar or remote training collar). As with any method of behavior modification, there are pros and cons. Ultimately, it's up to you to choose what method works best for you and your pets, so we've laid out the facts to help you decide.

I suggest NOT using these collars until your dog understands basic commands like sit and stay. That way you know that they comprehend what you are asking them to do and they can draw the association between any negative behavior and the "shock."

Best High-End Shock Collar: SportDOG FieldTrainer SD-425 Review

If you do decide that an e-collar is the right training device for your dog, we recommend the SportDOG FieldTrainer SD-425 for its 7 levels of correction, beep-only option, rechargeable battery and 500-yard range.

It's more expensive than some of the other electronic options out there, and it gives you more control and therefore a more positive training experience for your pup. It also allows you to train your dog with a much more mild tingle on 7 levels, rather than starting out with an intense shock. This is among our top picks for best dog training collar.

Best Budget Shock Collar: PetSpy M686 Premium Training Collar Review

If the SportDOG collar is out of your price range, the PetSpy M686 Premium Training Collar is another excellent option. It offers 4 training modes: vibration, sound, continuous and convulsive shock. And it gives you 8 adjustable levels of vibration and shock, so you can fine-tune the correction level.

I also like that this collar's contact points are made of conductive rubber to prevent skin irritation. It has a vast range (up to 1,000 feet), and the remote has a handy strap for easy portability. The adjustable collar fits most dogs (10-140 pounds), and the entire device is waterproof (but not remote).

How Does a Shock Collar Work?

Shock collars are a type of aversive training initially used in the 1960s to train hunting dogs. These days, shock collars are often used to curb a variety of stubborn and unwanted behaviors in family dogs, from excessive barking to food aggression, as well as to train pups to stay safely within a property line or to stick close by while off leash.

Shock collars are not intended as a punishment but more as a deterrent to negative or unsafe behavior. The theory is that your dog will associate the unwanted behavior with a slightly uncomfortable jolt and stop doing it until they no longer require the reminder.

The shock administered by an approved shock collar is safe, so while it is certainly enough to get your dog's attention and deter certain behaviors, it won't do any lasting physical harm.

With most shock collars, there are several levels of enforcement, so you can set the level to reprimand the unwanted behavior accordingly. For example, many shock collars will administer a beep or vibration as a warning before an actual shock is delivered to your dog. The beep also allows you to give a verbal command ("No!" or "Down!") with the warning beep or vibration to further disrupt the unwanted behavior.

With boundary training (often marketed as an electric or wireless fence), the shock collar is triggered by wires placed underground along the property line so the dog learns exactly how far they can go before they reach the boundary.

Once set to "shock" mode, there are usually varying levels of intensity delivered by a two-pronged device attached to a dog collar. If you're using a shock collar as a barking deterrent, the collar responds to the vibration of your dog's vocal cords. If you're using the collar to deter behavioral issues like food aggression, jumping or leash aggression, a remote control allows you to administer the shock in conjunction with the unwanted behavior.

Keep in mind, using a shock collar doesn't make you a bad pet parent, and it doesn't mean you are torturing your dog, especially when used on the lower non-shock levels. It is unlikely that an electronic training collar would destroy your relationship with your dog. In fact, shared training sessions could improve your bond with one another.

Here are four pros and four cons that we think everyone should consider before using or purchasing a shock collar for a dog.

Pros Of Shock Collars For Dogs

1. Adjustable Intensity

Most modern shock collars give you the flexibility of a warning beep or vibration mode, and adjustable shock level. This can be comforting to people who are on the fence about using a shock collar. Other collars, such as spray collars, which administer a harmless but foul-smelling blast up a dog's snout, are usually not adjustable.

2. Fast Results

Some pet owners report that it only took a few shocks to correct an unwanted behavior in their dog and after that, the beep or vibration was warning enough (for us we never even needed the shock at all). Shock collars can also be very effective at keeping your dog on your property, which will help keep them safe while giving them freedom. Of course, more stubborn dogs may take longer to train.

3. You Don't Need To Be Present

Shock collars, when used to control chronic barking, work even while you're away from home or inside the house.

This can be especially helpful if you've had neighbors complain about your dog's loud protests. The same goes for shock collars as boundary control, although they do require some hands-on training.

Personally, I would not leave my dog unattended with a shock collar as I would be scared of overcorrecting while I was not there to observe and adjust to the situation, but this is your choice. Also, we don't recommend leaving your dog unattended outside for extended periods of time, with or without a shock collar.

4. Affordable

A shock collar can be a cheaper alternative to a professional dog trainer or fence. Shock collars range in price from $30 to $250+, depending on features such as remote control, adjustable warning/shock levels, a range of distances (usually 30 to 400 yards), and the number of collars included.

Cons Of Shock Collars For Dogs

1. The Shock

Most pet owners can't fathom causing pain to their pet. But even with the ability to control the intensity of the correction, you are still using aversive behavior modification. Many dog trainers choose positive reinforcement (reward) as a means of behavior modification over negative feedback.

2. The Fear

Fear in dogs can be dangerous, so you never want to train a dog with fear. With shock training, some dogs may learn to fear people, objects, or situations they associate with the collar. One pet owner we know installed a wireless fence and then their dog refused to go outside after training with it. It even started urinating in the house instead of going to the back door to relieve itself in the yard.

3. Over-Correction

Without you there to control when a shock is administered, automatic bark collars and electric fences may deliver shocks unintentionally or too often. This unnecessary shock could confuse your dog by "correcting" a problem that was not even there.

4. No Positive Reward

On their own, shock collars don't reinforce good behavior with a positive reward such as your affection, verbal approval ("Good boy!") or a tasty treat. So while a shock collar may effectively deter negative behaviors like jumping on visitors or running after the mail carrier, it doesn't reward positive behavior such as sitting patiently or obeying a command to "Stay!". As with any training, you should always reinforce positive behavior with a reward of affection, playtime or a small treat.

Shock Collar Alternative: PetSafe Elite Outdoor Bark Control

 If you are seeking an alternative to the shock collar, try an ultrasonic bark control device. This one from PetSafe costs about $40 and looks like a birdhouse. It uses high-frequency ultrasonic sound to deter barking, which isn't harmful to pets.

It's weatherproof and for outside use. You can hang it on a tree, wall or fence to stop your dog or your neighbor's dog from obsessively barking. It's effective up to 50 feet away.

CHAPTER 12

Frequently Asked Questions

Can My Dog Sleep with a Cone On?

Yes – dogs can sleep, eat, drink, pee, and poop with a cone on. In fact, the stricter you are with the cone (officially called an Elizabethan collar or E-collar for short), the quicker your dog will get used to it. Plus, leaving the cone on at all times is one of the best ways to ensure they heal as quickly as possible.

Despite the stubbornly persistent myth that animal saliva speeds up healing, licking an incision is a sure way to interrupt the healing process. A dog licking their wound or chewing on their skin could cause them to inadvertently rip out their stitches, which could then reopen the incision or wound and introduce bacteria into it, which could cause a secondary infection.

Depending on how bad the damage is, treatment could require rinsing the open area, cutting out damaged tissue, and re-stitching the entire incision. The potential harm that can be done in a few minutes of "freedom" from the cone of shame is not worth the risk of causing more harm to your dog and ultimately prolonging their discomfort (not to mention the money that extra trip to the veterinarian is going to cost you).

By leaving the cone on when they're asleep (and in effect, when you're asleep and can't watch them), you 100% ensure this doesn't happen.

With that said, if your dog absolutely cannot stand the cone, there are certain E-collar alternatives (as well as tips and tricks) that can help make your dog more comfortable while still achieving the same purpose.

Luckily, in most cases, the E-collar (or some alternative to it) really only needs to be kept on your dog 7-10 days after surgery, which allows enough time for primary healing to occur. I promise, even if your dog seems to absolutely hate the cone of shame, they won't hold it against you in the long run– so stay strong and remember that keeping it on at all times is really the best and most loving thing you can do for them.

How Long Can My Dog Wear The E-Collar?

This is one of the more frequent questions from the dog owners. For those who use the e-collar for their dog, the most important thing they should be aware of is that the e-collar is a training device. It should be used only for training sessions and the dog can't wear it 24/7.

Below you can find several things that you will need to be mindful of while using the e-collar for your dog.

E-collar size

For the training sessions to be effective, you will need to ensure that the size of the e-collar suits your dog perfectly. If it feels tight around the dog's neck, it can cause them discomfort as the prongs might be poking the dog and cause an injury. On the other side, if the e-collar feels slack, then the contact points will not be touching the dog at all, rendering your efforts in using the e-collar to be useless.

As a general guide, always ensure that you can insert at most 2 fingers between the e-collar and the dog's neck. This will ensure that it fits the dog nicely and hence able to serve its intended purpose.

Settings on E-collar

Assuming that you have eased your dog into wearing the e-collar, the next important step that you will need to take is by knowing exactly what correction mode as well as the intensity of the stimulus that you should be using on the dog. This is an important step that most owners might miss out on! Some owners go about training the dog via the e-collar without knowing the limits of the collar.

If the above resonates with you, then it is high time you change your methodology and start to know what the correct settings are. For starters, always ensure that you start by adjusting the setting to its lowest. As you slowly, gradually increase the intensity, you will need to look at the dog's response to it before increasing it further.

Time of wearing the E-collar.

Last but not least, owners have the misconception that it is ok for the dog to wear the e-collar at all times. Unfortunately, this is a harmful practice that should be stopped. There are various reasons why you shouldn't do so. Let us find out what could go wrong if the dog wears the e-collar for prolonged periods, and how long can the dog wear the e-collar for.

What can happen if my dog wear an E-collar for prolonged periods?

If you left the e-collar on the dog for long periods in a day, it could cause bed sores or pressure necrosis on the dog's neck. With pressure necrosis, the skin around the affected area will gradually die off because blood cannot flow to the affected area due to the constriction of blood capillaries. It can also cause bed sores to the dog, and this is an excruciating process that no dogs should suffer from. Think of it as bedsore that bedridden patients suffer from after staying in bed for long periods.

If wearing the E-collar on the dog for long periods can cause damage to the dog's skin, what would be the maximum amount of time that the dog should be allowed to wear the e-collar?

As a general rule of thumb, the dog should not be wearing the e-collar uninterruptedly for more than 4 hours a day. Most of the time, owners flout this rule when they forget to take the e-collar off the dog, allowing their canine friend to wear the e-collar throughout the night. Hence, you will need to develop the habit of removing the training tool after each training session. When you do so, you can take the chance to inspect the dog's neck for any signs of pressure necrosis too.

Following these safety rules will provide you an excellent training time with your dog! 👍

CHAPTER 13

Dog Training Secrets

Repetition

Dogs are creatures of habit and learn by repetition. It may take several repitions of the same command before the response becomes implanted in the dogs brain and the action you are trying to teach him becomes automatic. Your dog will also require refresher sessions so that the command or action does not become lost during his life.

You should always praise him when he does something right.

Session length

Keep all training sessions short and enjoyable so that you dog's concentration is maintained throughout. Quality not quantity is the key, you should also always try to finish the training session on a positive note I you can.

Attitude

Always be reasonable in your expectations of what your dog can achieve. It takes time to get results. If your dog has difficulties in picking up a certain command try and look at why he is having difficulties. Come back to it another day.

Praise

Always use praise whenever you dog has successfully completed an exercise. This should also be done as soon as your dog has done the desired act (remember the section on timing) When delivering the praise look directly into his eyes so that he understand the connection between the voice or touch and his action. Deliver the praise either verbally or with the hand by either patting or stroking him.

Eye contact

Using eye contact can be more effective than using the spoken word especially if there is a close bond between the dog and owner. If a dog wishes to communicate with you he will look directly into your eyes trying to read your intent.

Hand Signals

Using specific hand signals while at the same time speaking to your dog can be an effective way of training you dog. It will be useful in getting young dog to respond at long distances and you can eventually stop the verbal commands so that he responds to the hand signal only. Give hand signal in front of and above the dog's head as this is in their line of vision.

Voice Signals

Dogs are known for their intelligence but they are only able to understand a few words, even those are more of an association between the sound you make and the action the dog has learned to respond to the sound with.

Use one command for one action and pronounce the command with the same tone of voice. You should gain your dogs attention by saying his name before starting a command.

It is important to realise that you dog will not understand every thing you say and may misunderstand the meaning of what you say. For example if you have trained you dog with the "down" command he may well if he is sitting on the furniture not respond to the command "get down" as he has only recognised the word down.